# Twenty Truths and a Lie



Elizabeth Donahue

BookLeaf Publishing

Presentation by *BookLeaf Publishing*

Web: www.bookleafpub.com

E-mail: info@bookleafpub.com

ISBN: 9789395950565

First edition 2022

*For C and D, always and forever.*

# Who Knew

When I was young, the words flowed so freely
Because I didn't know what they meant
Or how powerful they were.
And now, having lived and died a few times,
I can hardly speak
For fear of what I might make come true.
These harsh lessons learned, I saw them, I knew
Long before they were branded on my back.
No longer whispering trails of cloudy thoughts
Swirling inside my teenage mind,
Unformed and unrecognized
But now set free, made reality
With the flick of my own loaded pen.

# Dinner Plans

I'll be home a little late, you said.
Stopping for fresh vegetables on the way
At the farmstand where we always go.
But when I looked, the kitchen was empty,
Nothing cooking on the stove.
The little lies, they are the worst,
When they think that you don't know.

# My Advice

I never feel more myself
Than when I am being someone else.
I'm always telling the truth, I swear
When I hear myself lie and say I care.
I never smile brighter
Then when I feel dead inside.
And if I'm out and about it's because
There's nowhere else to hide.
How long can I keep this up?
I'll let you know when I fill my cup.
No one wants to hear this shit
So be strong girl, and just shut up.

# the gap

Blocked
Unrequested
Ghosted
Deleted
Unfriended
Canceled
All new words to say the same old thing
Whatever it was, it's over, my friend
And it was definitely you, not me.
I'm not sure how we got this way
Does anyone remember if I say
How it felt to be young on a summer night
Stars bursting with possibility?
Does anyone blindly reach for your hand on a walk
With no need for words to know it felt right?
Does anyone just speak from the heart in a fight?
It's been so long since anything felt real, I wonder
If my boys will know more than words on a screen
If they will be numb to it all, except in their dreams.
I don't pray much, but I'd beg on my knees

For their hearts to know true love, and heal from the cuts
Chests full of fresh air, clear water and rustling trees.

# long port

No matter how long it's been I can still see in my mind's eye
The view from the bridge that I crossed with you
When we were heading to our new life.
The water lapping at the shore, vibrating sapphires in the summer
Turned cold gray rocks by the end of fall.
My stomach full of butterflies when I would look over at you
Knowing we belonged
No matter what
And without taking your eyes off the road,
You would reach across and find me
And we would fly
Up the incline and over the crest
Down, away from the island to our little house in the woods.
Now I take back roads
I can hardly look at the signs
They were all wrong anyway
It wasn't the way home after all.

# Water Baby

My mother always tells the story
Of my first time at the beach.
It was a summer evening after a stormy day
Wind whipping
Waves crashing
Sand cool under our bare feet.
You took one look and screamed, she says.
Bloody murder, and jumped back in my arms,
Saying, let's go, let's leave, mommy please!
Are you going to just let her scream like that?
my grandfather said.
And Mom told him to stop.
She's just a baby,
And it's so loud,
She's just scared, for heaven's sake.
Isn't it funny, she always says,
That you grew up to love the beach so much?
And I thought that it was.

Crazy, that I always felt the pull of the tides
From every classroom seat
Undeniable, that I could taste the salt air
On every city street.
And when he brought me there, forever, he said,
My long journey was put to bed.

No more dreaming, no more fight
So grateful I had finally gotten it right.
But now I think back to that first time,
And wonder if it was a sign
Of all the pain that was yet to come.
I should have stayed where I was from.
It turned out that world of wind and waves was too wild
For a girl who wasn't raised on guile.

# Moment of Silence

Sitting on our front steps after dinner
One of the first real spring nights.
Our little triumvirate, eating ice cream in bowls.
What do you want to do this year, Mom? asks
my older son.
You know we can do anything we want to do.
Yes, I say, you're right, we can.
So let's think of what could be.
And Mom, he says, you don't have to be sad.
I know that Daddy passed away, but it's all right.
After a jolted moment, I ask, Do you know what
that means?
Yes, he says.
It means that person is no longer with you.
Daddy went away.
But I am here for you, and my brother too.
And I am stunned, by the pain of the blow
He didn't mean to strike
This little boy, turned too wise overnight.
Somberly too, the younger one takes my hand.
As the sky grows darker we plot and plan.
3 has always been my lucky number.

# You Have A New Message

Oh god here it comes
I was ready so many times before
Deeps breaths
Words prepared
Makeup done
But here it is
The awful truth
Hurtling at me at high speed
Technology's a wonder, as they say
I'm not dressed
The kids are right here
Cartoons blaring
It's not a good time
But the phone goes ding, and then once more
As much as I'd like, I can't ignore
The awful truth being typed my way.
Are you you?
Is he him?
If so, you might want to know.
And I'm so dumb, conditioned so well
I still ask
Does any of this ring a bell?
Oh god your face
When I say her name
You thought you'd be ready

Explanation at hand
Excuses in reach
Tell me I'm crazy again, oh please
But it caught you off guard
Like the truth always does
And now we can't pretend anymore.

# Photo Album

We were a work of art
Weren't we, though?
You and me
And then our two
Perfect bookends holding up a dream come true.
We touched pure joy, we knew sweet content
And no one, not even you,
Will ever tell me different.

# Soulmate

Nothing is sweeter than salt air to me
After the clouds have ambled out to sea
Nothing more clear than the mist of brine
Lingering while the waves kiss the shoreline.
A million times, over and over again
Like a lover whose devotion knows no end.
I'd rather watch them all night on the sand
Than wait for you to come hold my hand.

# Calendar

Summer was always mine,
And fall was always yours.
We split the year like dessert at a fancy
restaurant.
You sat in your chair on the beach
A grumpy old man
Tolerating all that fed my soul.
But I saw you smile, I swear, more than once
Because you saw me glowing
And you loved that.
And then one day, even before we both realized
It would be time.
And I would watch you come alive
Building your fires at night
Wood from your forest smoking and crackling
The red hot side of you finally exposed
To keep us all warm through the winter.
And I loved you more than that forgotten sun,
that endless beach, those incessant waves
I packed them away, like toys in a box
Neatly stored at the back of the closet.
Don't worry, I'd whisper, I'll find you again.
Sleep well all winter, my friends...
And I'd softly close the door on September,

So we could revel in the glory of you
And your season.

# Atsion Road

It takes about a hour
Round trip, I'd say
For me to send my children away.
Basics first
Sock and shoes?
Brush your teeth?
You need your hats and gloves today.
Got your bags?
Special toys?
I have to lock the door behind me.
We pile in.
Seatbelts clicked.
I never stop hating this.
It's just one turn and then we go
On our way down Atsion Road.
So many happy homes on our way
So many bikes in their driveways
Where no one has to make this trip.
We talk, of course, I stay cheerful
I cannot let them know I'm sick
Because it's not supposed to be this way.
Around the curve, farms come next
The first to spot a horse wins.
We pass the lake, and then the woods
Where we used to go all together

But I pray they don't remember.
The car grows quiet as we get closer
If they want to ask why, they don't.
One more turn and we are there.
They see his car and I hear them cheer
They are glad to see to see him here
As they should.
But it still kills me.
I pull in the spot, the doors fly open
I can barely steal a kiss goodbye
Before they are gone.
And it's time for me to do the long drive home alone
Battling back up Atsion Road
Fiddling with radio stations
Squeezing back tears
And wondering who wanted this anyway.

# Don't Look Down

A million little hells on earth
So many pockets of dread and despair
Open manholes around every corner
Keep your eyes peeled or suffer forever
That's what street signs should say.
You could be born into one
And have no say
Or be dragged into one
Because you cared too much
About the wrong person.
Lose track for a moment
And the landmine explodes
Forever altering your course
And searing your heart shut.
So many hells that no one sees coming
Until they are the one banging on the glass
Screaming at the top of their lungs,
But to everyone else, silently
Until they run out of air.
I can hardly believe
That we are supposed to fear another hell
Worse than this?
As if this punishment were not enough.

# Top 10 Hits

God, did you think that I loved you just because
I married you?
Toasting our anniversary is a fucking stupid
idea.
You're such a self-righteous bitch.
We were never a family.
It makes me so sad that you think I'm cheating.
She looks fat. (overheard)
I don't want to hold your hand, don't be such a
fucking baby.
I hate decorating the Christmas tree with you.
I wished you dead on that operating table.
I love you.

# World Series

The happiest night of my life, I can tell you exactly
Was early October
A Thursday, I'm sure
All windows open
Us on the couch
Our two babes snuggled up
The game on low
Glass of wine by our side
Your black socks pressed against my leg
I was silently cheering
We made it, we won!
The most valuable players
Our own party of four.
I swear on my life
I would never need anything more.
But little did I know
You'd thrown the game, laid down your bat
So convincing, your swing and a miss
No one would know it was on purpose
You made an end of our beginning
Long before the ninth inning.
I guess I can only hope
Your curse will last a hundred years too.

# Sunday Funday

When you find yourself
Hiding in your powder room
Clutching your child
Locking the door
Because wanting to go to a Superbowl party
with friends
Is now a punishable offense
It's time to go.

# Holidays

Happy New Year
Happy screw you year
All the worst of luck in the coming months
Pain, sadness, and misery too
I hope you survive on your diet of lies
Your vile, sordid hands have committed such crimes.
As I light the match and watch the flame
My wish is a spell that exposes your shame
And damns you to writhe in it eternally
So Happy New Year
Happy screw you year
Tonight I leave it all behind.

# In the Pines

These woods are so quiet
This lake is so still
It's been so long since I was in a peaceful place.
For many years
I thought I loved to fight the tides that could
drown me
I thought I loved to breathe the air that stung me
I thought I was made of stronger stuff
Until I was flung upon the rocks
And nearly drowned.
I made it out
But just barely.
Now I am content to walk in sand
That doesn't disappear beneath my feet.
I can cut through these ripples
On my own time
At my own speed
And without fear of reprimand.
I am older now
And wonder what would have happened, who I
would be
If I had lived here my whole life instead.

# Denial

Kiss me kiss me kiss me
Drown me so I forget
What I can barely comprehend
And never wanted to know.
Hold me tight, so I can run far away
To where I so desperately want to go.
Just for a few minutes there
I'll allow myself to believe you care
Even though I know you're poison.
You'll be gone before I wake
And I'll be the one who has to fake
That it was all for the best, I'll be okay.
When I would give anything for one more day
In denial.

# Disassociated

By the skin of my teeth
With last shred of my heart
I coasted in on fumes.
And now I am here
With no idea what to do
Because I never dreamed it would be without
you.
So I set down my bags
Get the lay of the land
And do my best impression of what a grown up
would do.
The audience is not buying it
So I've no other choices
Than to beg for redemption
State my name and rely on it
That I can become again who I used to be.
Trusting people is just not my strong suit these
days
Most of all, me.

# Birthday

21 is my day
I thought it belonged to you too
It was your number too after all
The one you wore when you were young
But one of the only true things I know
Is that we were a lie
It was supposed to be me and you against the world
But you were for you
First, last, and always.
It hasn't killed me
Yet
But I'm no wiser
No stronger
For it all.
Maybe next year.

www.ingramcontent.com/pod-product-compliance
Lightning Source LLC
Chambersburg PA
CBHW051759130826
49812CB00033B/1207
* 9 7 8 9 3 9 5 9 5 0 5 6 5 *